CRACK OPEN
KNOWLEDGE IN A NUTSHELL ON AMERICA --AND DISCOVER...

- Surprising facts about the "The Star-Spangled Banner"

- How the Pledge of Allegiance accidentally became a daily school tradition.

- How America got its name – by chance

- Why the White House was painted white

- The real Uncle Sam

i

CHARLES REICHBLUM

arpr, inc.
Paperbacks

Knowledge in a Nutshell® on America is the fourth book in the *Knowledge in a Nutshell®* series. Other books in this series are: *Knowledge in a Nutshell, Knowledge in a Nutshell on Sports*, and *Knowledge in a Nutshell on Popular Products Heinz Edition.*

CALL: 1-800-NUTSHELL (1-800-688-7435), or order through your local bookstore, amazon.com, barnesandnoble.com. e-book on our Web site:
www.knowledgeinanutshell.com

KNOWLEDGE IN A NUTSHELL® ON AMERICA

Copyright © 2001 by Knowledge in a Nutshell, Inc.

ISBN: 0-9660991-3-3

Printed in the United States of America by Geyer Printing Co., Pittsburgh, Pa.
arpr, inc. Paperbacks edition/November 2001
10 9 8 7 6 5 4 3 2 1

Dedication

- To all those who had the vision, hard work and good citizenship to make America a great nation.
- To those who fought to preserve America's freedoms.
- On a personal note, to my wife, our children: Bob, Diane, Bill and Amalie and our grandchildren, in chronological order: Rachel, Justin, Noah and Clarissa.
- To all those who helped produce this book, especially, our long-time administrative assistant, Barbara Rodi.
- To Jim Trusilo for the cover illustration, Bruce McGough and Noah Leibhart of Geyer Printing and Rob Handley and Tara Taylor of Droz and Associates for the cover design.
- To you my loyal readers, who have made the *Knowledge in a Nutshell*® series possible, thank you for your many wonderful comments.

CHAPTERS ON AMERICA

Preface

There are so many fascinating anecdotes about America, like the real story of the flag, how the Pledge of Allegiance accidentally became a daily school tradition, the stories-behind-the stories on the people who wrote the patriotic songs, why Washington, D.C. became the capital, why the White House is painted white—and even how America got its name, by chance.

Then there are those interesting, little-known facts about the U.S. Presidents, and the real Uncle Sam.

This is not meant to be a textbook. It's meant to be read, remembered and enjoyed.

You'll probably find things you never knew about America in this handbook about the country.

I hope you get as much pleasure as I did in discovering all this information about America.

ONE

Americana

One

AMERICANA

Surprising story
about the
White House

When the White House opened for the first time, in 1800, it wasn't white—and it wasn't called the White House.

It was built of gray sandstone and was grayish-brown in color.

Its name then was Executive Mansion or the President's House.

But in the last major foreign attack on the U.S. mainland before Sept. 11, 2001, the British invaded Washington during the War of 1812— and burned parts of the President's House.

Then to cover up the burn marks after the war, the house was painted white.

That's how the White House became white.

Gradually, people started calling it "The White House," although that name was not officially used until Theodore Roosevelt was President in the early 1900s.

The real
Uncle Sam

There was a man named Samuel Wilson who lived in Troy, New York.

He was a meat distributor, and was known around town as Uncle Sam.

When the War of 1812 started, Wilson provided meat for the Army—and stamped his nickname on barrels of salted meat.

A Troy newspaper published a report about how Uncle Sam Wilson was helping the war effort, and the story spread.

Before this time, the name Uncle Sam was not synonymous with the United States, but soldiers began saying that Uncle Sam was feeding the Army, and the name soon came to signify the United States as a whole.

The fact that the "U" and "S" of Uncle Sam's initials were the same as the "U" and "S" of United States made for a nice tie-in, and Uncle Sam became the nation's nickname.

Cartoonists started drawing pictures of Uncle Sam in clothes decorated with stars and stripes, and people everywhere began referring to the U.S. as Uncle Sam.

Finally, in 1961, Congress passed a resolution certifying Uncle Sam as a symbol for the United States.

Of all things—
a man named Flagg
makes the famous
Uncle Sam drawing

The most famous drawing of Uncle Sam was made by a man whose last name was appropriately, Flagg.

He was an American artist named James Montgomery Flagg.

Flagg drew Uncle Sam pointing his finger and saying, "I Want You."

Flagg had been a commercial illustrator for magazines and books, but nothing he ever did was as memorable as his Uncle Sam drawing— which really established Uncle Sam's appearance.

Other artists had drawn their interpretations of Uncle Sam but Flagg's drawing has become the standard.

The incredible coincidence of 2 American folk heroes

As noted, Sam Wilson became the inspiration for Uncle Sam—but in a surprising coincidence, his best friend when he was growing up was a boy named John Chapman—who would also become a legend.

John Chapman became known as Johnny Appleseed.

It was Chapman, a devoted horticulturist, who went around the country establishing apple orchards and selling apple seeds and apple trees.

Reportedly, he covered over 100,000 square miles of America, often walking barefoot, to spread his beloved apples.

Chapman had a religious fervor about him, and became famous as the barefoot evangelist of apples.

Actually he helped farmers wherever he went, and strengthened the economy, particularly throughout Ohio and Indiana. There's a monument to him in Mansfield, Ohio and a park named for him in Ft. Wayne, Indiana.

Amazingly, two boyhood playmates, John Chapman and Sam Wilson, both went down in American history under the names we know them by today—Johnny Appleseed and Uncle Sam.

The U.S. national bird --bald eagles— aren't really bald

The bald eagle was chosen as the national bird of the United States in 1782.

Despite their name, bald eagles actually are not bald. They only look that way because their heads are covered with white feathers.

The eagle was chosen as the national bird because they are native to North America and are symbols of power and freedom.

America could've had a different name

Amazingly, America got its name in a very unusual way.

In 1507, a long-forgotten German mapmaker, Martin Waldseemuller, made the first accepted map of the New World.

For reasons no one knows for sure today, he decided to name the New World after explorer Amerigo Vespucci.

But Waldseemuller easily could have picked another name. He could have chosen another explorer like Christopher Columbus or Leif Ericson. Or he could have in some way honored the native Indians who were here first.

Actually, Vespucci was an odd choice. Vespucci had explored only part of the coast of what is now South America. He had never visited any part of North America, and according to some historians, never left his ships to set foot on any part of the New World.

Then, there's the question of using first name or last name. Waldseemuller could have named the New World after Amerigo Vespucci's last name, and we could be called Vespucci today. And what if Waldseemuller had not altered Amerigo's first name slightly. We'd be Amerigo.

And, it was really by chance that Waldseemuller's map prevailed and was accepted. It's possible that some other mapmaker's work might have been the deciding one, and some other mapmaker might have picked a different name for America.

4 states
almost had
different names

Vermont was almost going to be called New Connecticut, and in fact, used that name for a short time in the 1700s.

Colorado was originally going to be Jefferson.

The state of Washington came close to being called Columbia.

West Virginia was thinking about naming their state Kanawha, after the river of that name in their state.

U.S. soldiers not always called GIs

The custom of calling U.S. servicemen and women GIs didn't begin until World War II.

The initials came from "government issue," describing the uniform and equipment given to them.

But in World War I, American soldiers were called Doughboys. The name Doughboys became popular because they were served so much doughy food in those days.

Father and son win Medal of Honor

The Medal of Honor is the highest military award for bravery given to any member of the U.S. Armed Forces.

Among the select number of people who have won the Medal is a father-son combination.

General Douglas MacArthur was awarded the Medal of Honor in World War II, and his father, Arthur MacArthur, had received it for service in the Civil War.

He works out of
his house

Did you ever stop to think that the person with the biggest job in the world works out of his house.

That person is the President of the United States.

Surprising size
of White House

It doesn't look that big from the outside, but the White House has 132 rooms.

Included in the house are an indoor swimming pool, tennis court, gymnasium and movie theater.

The State Dining Room can seat up to 120 dinner guests.

Why the dollar sign looks like it does

The U.S. dollar sign came from the initials of the country.

The dollar sign was originally created by taking the "S" from U.S., and superimposing the "U" over it.

Eventually, the bottom part of the U was dropped and the two lines in the U are now often replaced with just one line.

How Veterans Day started

Until the early 1950s, Nov. 11 was known as Armistice Day, honoring World War I veterans.

But a merchant in Emporia, Kansas, Alvin King, led efforts to change the name to Veterans Day to recognize all U.S. veterans.

King lobbied to push the idea through Congress—and Veterans Day became a national day of recognition in 1954.

The Presidents
in their 40s

Eight men became President of the United States before they were 50 years old.

They were Theodore Roosevelt who became President at 42, John Kennedy at 43, Bill Clinton at 46, Ulysses Grant at 46, Grover Cleveland at 47, Franklin Pierce at 48, James Polk at 49 and James Garfield at 49.

13-year-old
designs state flag

Alaska ran a contest for someone to design its state flag.

The winner was a 13-year-old boy, Benny Benson.

His design is still used today.

Lots of
ones

Would you believe the word or number "one" appears on a U.S. one-dollar bill in 16 different places.

At first glance, most people can't find all 16 "ones," but to help you, here they are:

On the front of the bill there are four "ones" in figures on the four corners. The word "one" appears at the bottom of the bill and on the right side in the middle of the bill. That's six on the front.

On the four corners of the back, there are eight "ones"—four in figures and four in words—plus the word "one" in the middle and bottom of the bill.

That's 10 on the back, for a total of 16.

No pennies

Everybody calls the U.S. one-cent piece a penny, but the word "penny" doesn't appear anywhere on the coins.

The hot and
cold of it

The hottest outdoor temperature ever recorded in the U.S. was 134 degrees Fahrenheit.

That happened at Death Valley, California, on July 10, 1913.

Coldest day ever in the U.S. was 80 below zero at Prospect Peak, Alaska, on Jan. 23, 1971.

The coldest day in any state except Alaska was 70 below at Rogers Pass, Montana, on Jan. 20, 1954.

A snowy
day

The record for the most snow in one day in the U.S. was set at Silver Lake, Colorado, on April 14, 1921.

It snowed 76 inches in 24 hours.

How could a man be born in Florida AND Missouri

The famous author, Mark Twain, was indeed born in Florida and Missouri.

How's that possible?

Twain was born in the town of Florida, Missouri.

Those men named Francis

By coincidence, the men who wrote "The Star-Spangled Banner," "My Country 'Tis of Thee," and the Pledge of Allegiance to the Flag, plus the man who most historians credit with making the first American flag, all had first or middle names of Francis.

Francis Scott Key wrote "The Star-Spangled Banner," Samuel Francis Smith wrote "My Country 'Tis of Thee," Francis Bellamy wrote the Pledge of Allegiance, and Francis Hopkinson is credited with making the first flag.

Tallest
structure

The tallest structure in the U.S. is not in any big city.

The tallest is a TV tower in Blanchard, North Dakota.

That North Dakota tower is 2,063 feet high, or almost 800 feet higher than the Empire State Building.

Brothers and
Sisters

There's one U.S. state that has towns named Brothers and Sisters.

Both towns are in Oregon.

Only one state
named for President

Surprisingly, of all of the 50 states in the U.S., only one is named after a President.

You'd think there would have been more, but the only state named for a President is Washington.

How old must you be
to serve as President or
in Congress

According to the Constitution, a person must be at least 35 years old to be President.

U.S. Senators must be at least 30, and members of the House of Representatives, 25.

Win a bet
on money

Although we handle money all the time, amazingly few people can answer this question correctly:

Name the person pictured on each of these denominations of U.S. money—the $5, $10, $20 and $50 bills.

Answer: On the $5 is Abraham Lincoln. On the $10, Alexander Hamilton. On the $20, Andrew Jackson. On the $50, Ulysses Grant.

All were Presidents except Hamilton who was the first Secretary of the Treasury.

There she is,
Miss America

The first Miss America contest was held in 1921, and the first winner was Margaret Gorman from Washington, D.C.

Then Mary Catherine Campbell of Ohio won the Miss America title two straight years, in 1922 and 1923.

Surprisingly, there was no rule then against the same woman winning more than once.

The shortest address
makes the
longest impression

On Nov. 19, 1863, ceremonies were held at the site of the Battle of Gettysburg in Pennsylvania, dedicating part of the battlefield as a cemetery for those who lost their lives in that Civil War battle.

Although Abraham Lincoln, the President of the United States, was there, the main speaker that day was Congressman Edward Everett.

Everett spoke for two hours.

By the time it was Lincoln's turn to speak, some spectators had already left.

Finally, Lincoln stood up—and delivered one of the greatest speeches of all time.

Nobody today can recall what Everett said in his two hours, but Lincoln—in about two minutes—gave his immortal Gettysburg Address that still stirs deep, inspirational feelings.

His closing words were, "this government of the people, by the people, for the people, shall not perish from the earth."

The man who
named the USA

As we mentioned earlier in this chapter, a German mapmaker in the 1500s came up with the name America.

But who gave the country its full name of United States of America?

Until 1776, that name did not exist.

The country was known as "The Colonies", or the "United Colonies," or "The American Colonies."

Thomas Paine, who was famous for writing "Common Sense," a pamphlet urging independence from England, made the suggestion that the new nation be called the United States of America.

The Continental Congress waited 67 days after the announcement of the Declaration of Independence to adopt a name for the country.

Conceivably, they could have picked something else, but on Sept. 9, 1776 they took Paine's idea and officially declared "The United States of America" to be the nation's name.

TWO

The Flag
and Pledge of Allegiance

Two

THE FLAG

The mystery of
the U.S. flag

As important as the flag of the United States is to the nation, it's amazing that no one really knows who designed it.

The long-time legend about Betsy Ross is disputed by many historians.

According to the legend, George Washington and two Congressmen called on Ross in May, 1776. She was a widowed upholsterer in Philadelphia, and so the story goes, she agreed to design and sew the first flag.

But the story is in doubt for two reasons.

There is no verification, written record or proof that the meeting with Washington and the Congressmen actually happened, and the story was promoted years later by Ross' grandson who claimed his grandmother told him how she made the first official U.S. flag.

There is a famous painting by Charles Weisgerber showing Betsy Ross sewing a flag. The painting was made in the late 1800s and may

The Flag

have been based on Ross' grandson's account.

But, there is more evidence that a man named Francis Hopkinson really designed the first flag.

He was a Philadelphia judge who was also an artist and did design a naval flag. He went so far as to send a bill to the Continental Congress for his services for making the first U.S. flag. He asked for a "quarter cask of wine" as compensation.

There's no record that the Continental Congress gave him the wine, but they did name him as the designer of the flag in their official journals, although they noted that others were consulted on the design.

So the mystery of the origin of the U.S. flag continues.

Flag etiquette

Congress has established rules for the correct display and handling of the American flag.

Flying the flag outdoors...The flag is customarily flown only from sunrise to sunset— but it may be flown at night on special occasions if properly lighted. Some places customarily fly the flag outdoors 24 hours a day, such as the White House, Capitol, Ft. McHenry in Baltimore where "The Star-Spangled Banner" was written, and at U.S. Customs ports of entry.

Displaying the flag indoors...In an auditorium, the flag may be displayed flat, above and behind the speaker. When displayed on a staff in an auditorium, church, etc., it should be at the speaker's right as he or she faces the audience. Any other flag should be at the speaker's left. When the flag is displayed on a wall, the stars should be at the top and at the observer's left. When used to cover a casket, the flag should be placed so the stars are at the head and over the left shoulder. The flag should not be lowered into a

37

grave.

Half staff...The flag should be hoisted first to the top, then lowered to half-staff. When taking it down, it again should be hoisted to the top before being lowered.

Prohibited uses...The flag should never be displayed with the stars down except as a distress signal. It should never be displayed on an automobile, boat or float except from a staff. It should not have any words placed on it. The flag should never be allowed to touch the ground or floor.

Saluting the flag...The proper way for those not in military uniform to honor the flag when it is passing in a parade, during a hoisting or lowering ceremony, when the national anthem is played, and for the Pledge of Allegiance, is to place the right hand over the heart. Men should remove hats and place them over their hearts. Those in military uniform should salute.

More than
13 stripes

For many years the U.S. flag has had 13 stripes and as many stars as there are states in the Union.

But there was a time when a new stripe was added each time a new state entered the Union.

When the 14th and 15th states, Vermont and Kentucky, were admitted in the 1790s, two stripes were added to the original 13, and the flag had 15 stripes.

However, it dawned on members of Congress that the flag would become unwieldy if there was a new stripe for each new state.

So Congress then took away the 14th and 15th stripes and passed a law that the U.S. flag would always stay at 13 stripes to honor the original 13 states, and only new stars would be put on the flag for new states.

Why red,
white and blue?

The U.S. had no official flag during the early years of the Revolutionary War, and troops carried flags of different designs—with different colors—into battles.

Finally, on June 14, 1777, the Continental Congress passed a resolution authorizing the red, white and blue flag with stars and stripes as the official flag of the United States.

A later resolution said the colors were chosen to designate:

* Red for hardness and courage

* White for purity and innocence

* Blue for vigilance, perseverance and justice

That famous flag picture

It's been called one of the greatest newspaper photos ever made.

On Feb. 23, 1945, an American patrol captured Mt. Suribachi on Iwo Jima during World War II.

Six servicemen then fastened the U.S. flag to an old pipe lying nearby, and raised it.

An Associated Press war photographer named Joe Rosenthal happened to be there. He took the picture, and it inspired the nation.

Rosenthal won a Pulitzer prize for the photo, and the Marine Corps War Memorial across the Potomac River from Washington is based on the picture.

Fifty-six years later, in September, 2001, firefighters at the World Trade Center replicated the raising of the flag on a bent steel rod.

Who wrote the
Pledge of Allegiance
To the Flag?

For many years there was a dispute about who wrote the Pledge of Allegiance.

The Pledge first appeared in Youth's Companion, a weekly magazine, in 1892.

The magazine originally said the Pledge was written by one of their executives, James Upham.

But later, Francis Bellamy, a writer for the magazine, claimed he was the author.

In 1939, the U.S. Flag Association appointed a committee to study the controversy and they upheld Bellamy's claim.

The Library of Congress now recognizes Bellamy as the author.

Two changes have been made in the Pledge since it was first published.

Thirty years after it first appeared, the words "flag of the United States of America" replaced the phrase "my flag."

And in 1954, an Act of Congress added the words "under God."

The current version of the Pledge is:

I pledge allegiance to the flag of the United States of America and to the republic for which it stands, one nation under God, indivisible, with liberty and justice for all.

How the Pledge
entered the schools

The Pledge of Allegiance became a daily part of school life in America—accidentally.

In 1892, President Benjamin Harrison ordered a National School Celebration Day to mark the 400th anniversary of Columbus' voyage to America.

Someone called Harrison's attention to the Pledge, which had just been written. As an afterthought, Harrison said part of the Columbus celebration could be the reciting of the Pledge in schools across the country.

Once that special celebration ended, schools continued to have students say the Pledge every morning, and the tradition was born.

43

THREE

The Songs

Three

THE SONGS

"God Bless America"

The amazing thing about the inspiring song "God Bless America" is that it sat in a desk drawer—unsung—for 20 years after it was written.

Irving Berlin wrote "God Bless America" in 1918 for a Broadway show, "Yip, Yip, Yaphank." But during rehearsals, the show was running long, and the song was eliminated.

Berlin regretfully stuck the sheet music in the bottom of his desk drawer, and there it sat for 20 years, never heard by the public.

Finally, in 1938, with World War II looming, singer Kate Smith asked Berlin if he could give her a patriotic song for her network radio program.

Berlin went to his old desk and eagerly dug out the copy of "God Bless America."

Smith introduced it, and it immediately became one of the most cherished songs in the

The Songs

nation's history.

But that's only part of the story...Berlin grew up poor. He had to leave school after only a few years to go to work and help support his family. He sold newspapers on the Lower East Side of New York City and sang for money on street corners.

Eventually, he became a singing waiter and began writing songs. By the time he was 23, he had his first hit, "Alexander's Ragtime Band," in 1911.

Over the next seven years he had other hits. In 1918 he wanted to express his gratitude to his country—and he wrote his love song to America.

His opening words, "God Bless America, land that I love," so touched Berlin that he refused to ever take any money from the song. He donated all royalties to the Boy and Girl Scouts for the rest of his life.

"America the Beautiful"

A 33-year-old teacher, Katharine Lee Bates, wrote the words to the song, "America the Beautiful."

Ms. Bates was inspired to write it after visiting Pikes Peak, Colorado, by chance, while on vacation in 1893.

She was so enthralled with the view, she immediately wrote down the first draft of the words before returning home to her job as an English teacher at Wellesley College in Massachusetts.

The melody, added later, was from Samuel Ward's hymn, "Materna."

Her words:

O beautiful for spacious skies,
For amber waves of grain.
For purple mountain majesties,
Above the fruited plain.
America! America!
God shed His grace on thee.
And crown thy good with brotherhood,
From sea to shining sea.

The Songs

O beautiful for pilgrim feet
Whose stern impassion'd stress
A thorough-fare for freedom beat
Across the wilderness.
America! America!
God mend thine ev'ry flaw,
Confirm thy soul in self control,
Thy liberty in law.

O beautiful for heroes prov'd
In liberating strife,
Who more than self their country lov'd
And mercy more than life.
America! America!
May God thy gold refine
Till all success be nobleness,
And ev'ry gain divine.

O beautiful for patriot dream
That sees beyond the years,
Thine alabaster cities gleam,
Undimmed by human tears.
America! America!
God shed His grace on thee,
And crown thy good with brotherhood
From sea to shining sea.

Surprising facts about
"The Star-Spangled Banner"

Most everyone knows that Francis Scott Key wrote "The Star-Spangled Banner" while watching America's defense of Ft. McHenry in the War of 1812—but there's so much more to the story.

Key was in Baltimore on Sept. 13, 1814 when the British were trying to capture the fort. They bombarded it almost all night. When dawn came on Sept. 14, Key and other American observers did not know who had won the battle because the smoke and haze was so thick.

Suddenly, at 7 a.m., the haze cleared for a moment—and they saw the American flag was still flying over the fort.

Key was so excited, he pulled an envelope out of his pocket and started writing his emotional words, "Oh say can you see, by the dawn's early light, what so proudly we hailed at the twilight's last gleaming? Whose broad stripes and bright stars, through the perilous fight...gave proof through the night that our flag was still there."

Minutes later, he wrote the complete first

The Songs

stanza, then later in the day wrote all four stanzas.

The next day, Key gave his poem to his brother-in-law, Judge J.H. Nicholson, who had the words printed on handbills and distributed throughout Baltimore. On Sept. 20, a Baltimore newspaper printed the four verses.

It was still not a song.

But a few days later, an actor, Ferdinand Durang, sang Key's words. Durang put the words to an old English drinking tune, "To Anacreon in Heaven."

Durang's rendition of the song was well received, and the song's popularity began to spread around the Baltimore area, and eventually around the country.

One of the surprises is that Key had given it a different name when he wrote it. He called it "The Defense of Fort McHenry," but later changed the title to "The Star-Spangled Banner."

Key was not a professional writer. He was a lawyer. He practiced law for many years in Maryland and Washington, D.C. It was his thrill of seeing the flag still standing that inspired him to write his verses.

The biggest surprise of all about "The Star-Spangled Banner" is that it was NOT made the national anthem until 1931. That's when Congress voted to make it the official anthem of the country—117 years after it was written.

Here are all four of Key's stanzas:

I

Oh, say can you see by the dawn's early light
What so proudly we hailed at the twilight's last gleaming?
Whose broad stripes and bright stars thru the perilous fight,
O'er the ramparts we watched were so gallantly streaming?
And the rocket's red glare, the bombs bursting in air,
Gave proof through the night that our flag was still there.
Oh, say does that star-spangled banner yet wave
O'er the land of the free and the home of the brave?

The Songs

II

On the shore, dimly seen through the mists of
the deep,
Where the foe's haughty host in dread silence
reposes,
What is that which the breeze, o'er the towering
steep,
As it fitfully blows, half conceals, half discloses?
Now it catches the gleam of the morning's first
beam,
In full glory reflected now shines in the stream:
'Tis the star-spangled banner! Oh long may it
wave
O'er the land of the free and the home of the
brave!

III

And where is that band who so vauntingly
swore
That the havoc of war and the battle's confusion,
A home and a country should leave us no more!
Their blood has washed out their foul footsteps'
pollution.

No refuge could save the hireling and slave
From the terror of flight, or the gloom of the grave:
And the star-spangled banner in triumph doth wave
O'er the land of the free and the home of the brave!

IV

Oh! Thus be it ever, when freemen shall stand
Between their loved home and the war's desolation!
Blest with victory and peace, may the heav'n rescued land
Praise the Power that hath made and preserved us a nation.
Then conquer we must, when our cause it is just,
And this be our motto: "In God is our trust."
And the star-spangled banner in triumph shall wave
O'er the land of the free and the home of the brave!

The minister
who wrote
"My Country 'Tis of Thee"

The Rev. Samuel Francis Smith was a Baptist clergyman in Boston when he wrote the words to "My Country 'Tis of Thee," which is also called "America."

Oddly enough, the music he chose for his song was the melody of the British national anthem, "God Save the King (Queen)," and also the same melody used at that time for the German national anthem.

"My Country 'Tis of Thee" was first sung in public on July 4, 1831 at a children's picnic at the Park Street Church in Boston.

Since this was long before either "God Bless America" or "America the Beautiful" was written, "My Country 'Tis of Thee" became the second-most popular patriotic song in the country after "The Star-Spangled Banner." It was heard far more often in those days than it is today.

But the Reverend Smith's words are still inspiring and many have never heard all 4 stanzas:

The Songs

My country 'tis of thee,
Sweet land of liberty,
Of thee I sing.
Land where my fathers died!
Land of the Pilgrims' pride!
From ev'ry mountainside,
Let freedom ring!…
My native country, thee,
Land of the noble free,
Thy name I love.
I love thy rocks and rills,
Thy woods and templed hills;
My heart with rapture thrills
Like that above…
Let music swell the breeze,
And ring from all the trees
Sweet freedom's song.
Let mortal tongues awake;
Let all that breathe partake;
Let rocks their silence break,
The sound prolong…
Our fathers' God, to Thee,
Author of liberty,
To Thee we sing.
Long may our land be bright
With freedom's holy light;
Protect us by Thy might,
Great God, our King!

Yankee Doodle
Dandy

The first patriotic song in America was "Yankee Doodle."

American troops adopted "Yankee Doodle" during the Revolutionary War and often whistled it in battle.

When the British left after their surrender at Yorktown, ending the war, U.S. bands rubbed it in by serenading them with the song.

In effect, "Yankee Doodle" was the U.S. national anthem at that time, although it had no official status.

Actually, the song had no American origin. It was an old tune believed to have come from southern Europe in the Middle Ages. It then became popular in Holland and England with varying words.

The English added the curious words about sticking a feather in a cap and calling it macaroni that poked fun at English men of the time who dressed in Italian styles.

The American version of the words were

written by an army surgeon, Dr. Richard Schuckburgh in the 1750s.

The words Schuckburgh wrote don't seem particularly inspiring or patriotic today, but they were a big hit then. His lyrics:

"Father and I went down to camp,
along with Captain Goodwin,
And there we saw the men and boys,
as thick as hasty puddin'
Yankee Doodle keep it up.
Yankee Doodle dandy,
Mind the music and the step,
And with the girls be handy."

The song became so identified with the U.S. that people in other countries started calling Americans "Yankees" or "Yanks."

Oddly, in America itself, southerners eventually used the word Yankee only for northerners, and many northerners used it only for people from New England.

The other oddity is that the word Yankee originally had nothing to do with America. Authorities say it came from either the Scottish word "yankie" or the Dutch "Jan Kees."

The real
Yankee Doodle
Dandy

One hundred and three years after the Revolutionary War began, George M. Cohan was born in Providence, Rhode Island, on July 3, 1878—although in later years he always said he was born on the 4th of July.

Cohan took the old song "Yankee Doodle," changed the words and music, and made it into one of the biggest hits of all time.

He called it "Yankee Doodle Dandy," with near-autobiographical lyrics—"I'm a Yankee Doodle Dandy, a Yankee Doodle, do or die; A real live nephew of my Uncle Sam's, Born on the Fourth of July."

The 1942 Academy Award-winning movie based on his life was named "Yankee Doodle Dandy," with James Cagney playing Cohan.

Cohan wrote other patriotic songs like "You're a Grand Old Flag," and during World War I, he inspired American troops and the nation with "Over There." That song included:

"Over there, over there
Send the word, send the word over there,
That the Yanks are coming, the Yanks
are coming
The drums rum-tumming everywhere.
…So prepare, say a prayer,
Send the word, send the word to beware.
We'll be over, we're coming over,
And we won't come back till it's over,
over there."

Cohan was the son of vaudevillians and performed with his mother, father and sister. By age 16 he was writing his own songs and then branched into Broadway shows where he was an actor, writer, director and producer. Many of his shows had an All-American slant.

President Franklin Roosevelt honored Cohan for his patriotic songs with a special medal.

Besides the movie "Yankee Doodle Dandy," his life and songs were also the basis for a 1968 Broadway musical, "George M!" The famous "M" in his name stood for Michael.

FOUR

The Treasures

Four

THE TREASURES

The 19 words that galvanized America

When 39-year-old Patrick Henry rose to speak on March 23, 1775, he was to deliver—as it turned out—one of the greatest speeches of all time.

People had always cried out for freedom, but nobody expressed it better than Henry that day.

America was on the brink of war with England. Some people thought the war for freedom should be fought; some didn't.

Henry said, "I know not what course others may take; but as for me, give me liberty or give me death!"

Those 19 words helped inspire Americans to go forward and create an independent, free nation.

"Who shall write the Declaration of Independence?"

By June of 1776, the Continental Congress decided America should formally declare its freedom—and the document they produced turned out to be one of the most stirring in history.

The process started when Richard Henry Lee stood up in Congress and made a motion that a declaration of independence for the American colonies should be written. "We ought to be free," he famously said.

Congress passed the motion and appointed a committee to draft a declaration.

The committee consisted of John Adams, Thomas Jefferson, Benjamin Franklin, Roger Sherman and Robert Livingston.

The committee's first order of business was, "Who shall write the declaration?"

On June 11 they gave the job to 33-year-old Thomas Jefferson.

Working day and night, Jefferson wrote the Declaration of Independence in less than three weeks.

It was sent back to Congress on June 28,

approved on July 2, and declared on July 4.

The first person to sign the Declaration was the president of the Continental Congress, John Hancock. He became famous for writing his name big and bold. That led to the tradition of people saying even today that when someone signs a document, they put their "John Hancock" on it.

Many of the phrases Jefferson dashed off in the Declaration of Independence had a lasting, profound influence on the future of America, and gave inspiration to others in the world.

Among his immortal words were, "We hold these truths to be self-evident, that all men are created equal, that they are endowed by their Creator with certain unalienable Rights, that among these are Life, Liberty and the Pursuit of Happiness."

The Declaration of Independence remains one of the great historic landmarks.

That is Jefferson's, and America's gift to humankind.

A roomful
of giants

A group of 55 men met in Philadelphia in May, 1787.

The purpose of their meeting was to write what is now the Constitution of the United States.

They worked all through a hot summer, not finishing until September 17.

What a roomful of giants it was.

The oldest person there was the wise Benjamin Franklin, then 81. Other greats included George Washington, James Madison, Alexander Hamilton.

The most amazing feature of their work was this:

Here were 55 human beings, meeting more than 200 years ago without knowing the vast changes that were to come to the world over the next two centuries; yet they were able to write a document that is as brilliant and workable today as it was then.

America was lucky that people of that caliber were there. They were creating a new form of government—one the world had never seen before.

They argued. They compromised. They fought for principles. And they wound up with one of the great documents of all time.

In their preamble, they talked about forming a more perfect Union. And they did. Here is the complete preamble:

"We the people of the United States, in order to form a more perfect Union, establish justice, insure domestic tranquility, provide for the common defense, promote the general welfare, and secure the blessings of liberty to ourselves and our posterity, do ordain and establish this Constitution for the United States of America."

The tradition of
Freedom of Religion

If you read the Bill of Rights in the U.S. Constitution, the very first words you see are:

"Congress shall make no law respecting an establishment of religion, or prohibiting the free exercise thereof."

It's significant that the first thing mentioned in the Bill of Rights centers on Freedom of Religion because that is what brought many early settlers to America, long before the Constitution was written.

For example, the Pilgrims came to America in 1620 expressly to escape religious persecution abroad. Others seeking religious freedom followed.

The great gift these people gave was the idea that America was a land where people could worship as they pleased.

The tradition had started, and became guaranteed in the Constitution.

13 years—
3 great documents

The place: The House of Representatives during the first session of the First Congress. The date: Sept. 9, 1789. The Congressman from Virginia, James Madison proposes additions to the Constitution.

The result: The Bill of Rights.

They consist of just 10 short paragraphs, but what they say creates a whole way of life— freedom of speech, press, religion; right to petition, speedy trial, witnesses, counsel; due process of law; right to security against unreasonable search and seizure.

In just 13 years, from 1776 to 1789, a handful of men wrote three of the greatest documents in history—the Declaration of Independence, the Constitution and the Bill of Rights—which have contributed so much to the heritage of the United States.

A national treasure
for $300

One of the great icons of America—the Liberty Bell—was purchased for about $300.

Pennsylvania had originally ordered the bell from England in 1752 to proclaim legislative meetings. But when the Declaration of Independence was adopted in Philadelphia in 1776, the bell was rung to announce the joyous event.

It was then rung every July 4 thereafter until 1835.

Contrary to popular opinion, its famous crack did not happen when it was proclaiming liberty.

The crack occurred when tolling for the funeral of John Marshall, Chief Justice of the U.S., in 1835.

The inscription on the bell is from the Bible (Leviticus 25:10), "Proclaim Liberty throughout all the land unto all inhabitants thereof."

Although it can't be rung anymore, the bell is still on display in Philadelphia.

The tallest Memorial

The Washington Monument is the tallest structure honoring an American President.

Located near the Potomac River, about halfway between the Capitol and the Lincoln Memorial, it stands 555 feet high.

Some people wanted to honor George Washington with a monument while he was alive, but he objected to the expense. Forty years after his death, groups were organized to raise funds, and following many financial and construction delays the monument was finally dedicated in 1885.

Visitors who want to forego the elevator can walk to the top. There are 898 steps.

60-foot-high
faces

A sculptor, Gutzon Borglum, worked 14 years, from 1927 to 1941, supervising the carving of four U.S. Presidential faces on Mt. Rushmore in the Black Hills of South Dakota—but he died before the job was finished.

The four Presidential faces are those of Washington, Jefferson, Lincoln and Theodore Roosevelt.

Finally, the job was completed under the direction of his son whose first name was, appropriately, Lincoln.

The faces are each about 60 feet high—the largest in the nation.

The noses are 20 feet long, mouths, 18 feet wide and the eyes are 11 feet across.

The luck
of 13

Although 13 is supposed to be an unlucky number, the U.S. ignored that superstition in designing the official Great Seal of the United States.

There are an incredible number of 13s connected with the Seal.

The eagle on the Seal has 13 feathers and holds an olive branch of 13 leaves and 13 olives in its right talon, and 13 arrows in its left.

Also on the Seal are 13 stars and 13 stripes and 13 sections of a pyramid.

Inscribed is E Pluribus Unum—which has 13 letters.

And the man who designed the Seal, William Barton, had 13 letters in his name.

The National
Motto

Congress waited all the way until 1956 to designate an official national motto for the nation.

In that year, they declared the national motto to be "In God We Trust."

The first use of "In God We Trust" by the government was when it was placed on some coins during the Civil War.

But then it disappeared and reappeared on various coins randomly until 1955 when Congress ordered it placed on all U.S. coins and paper money.

The woman's face
on the Statue of Liberty

Although the face on the Statue of Liberty is one of the most famous in the world, few know whose face it is.

The statue was designed by a French sculptor, Frederic Bartholdi—and he used his mother, Charlotte, as the model. He said his mother's face was perfect because she looked strong and honest.

Charlotte Bartholdi has been immortalized even though her name is not well known.

The statue, a gift from the French people to the United States, was dedicated on October 28, 1886.

Its torch, held high, symbolizes liberty shedding light upon the world. At her feet is a broken shackle, symbolizing the overthrow of tyranny.

For over 100 years the statue has served as an inspiration to Americans and others yearning to be free.

Why the French
gave America
the Statue

France presented the Statue of Liberty to America as a symbol of the liberty that citizens enjoy under a democratic government.

America's example of liberty helped pave the way for the French Revolution which brought democracy to France.

The French people donated about $250,000 for the building of the statue, and Americans raised about $280,000 for the pedestal and installation.

A smaller model can be seen in France, standing on a bridge over the Seine River in Paris.

The emotional poem
at the Statue of Liberty

The poem now engraved on the pedestal of the Statue of Liberty was written by a 34-year-old poet from New York, in 1883, Emma Lazarus.

But after Ms. Lazarus wrote it, it was forgotten for 20 years and was not attached to the statue until 1903.

Ms. Lazarus, who died at 38, never knew it became part of the Statue of Liberty.

The last lines of the poem are:

"Give me your tired, your poor,
Your huddled masses yearning to breathe free…
Send these, the homeless, tempest-tossed to me,
I lift my lamp beside the golden door!

FIVE

The Fun Facts on the Presidents

Five

THE PRESIDENTS

George Washington
1st President

President, April 30, 1789 to March 3, 1797...Took office at age 57, left at 65...College: None...Party: Federalist...VP: John Adams... Although called the "Father of the Country," he had no children of his own...Only President never to live in White House (it wasn't built yet)...Dropped out of school at age 14...An attack of smallpox early in his life left scars on his face...His wife, Martha, was one of richest women in Virginia...Was against naming the capital Washington, D.C. (he preferred "Federal City")...Probably most popular President of all time. Rarely, if ever, criticized during or after his Presidency...Only President elected unanimously by the Electoral College for both terms.

John Adams
2nd President

President, March 4, 1797 to March 3, 1801...Took office at age 61, left at 65...College: Harvard...Party: Federalist...VP: Thomas Jefferson...Although he played significant role in America's independence, and was highly intelligent, his lack of charisma doomed his popularity and stature while in office and for many years after (only recently have historians given him his due)...Was so bitter at losing his reelection bid for a second term to Jefferson, he refused to attend Jefferson's Inauguration ceremonies...Until the year 2001, Adams held the record as longest-living President (he lived 90 years, 247 days—a record finally broken by Ronald Reagan who reached 90 years, 248 days in October, 2001).

Thomas Jefferson
3rd President

President from March 4, 1801 to March 3, 1809…Took office at age 57, left at 65…College: William & Mary…Party: Democratic-Republican…VPs: Aaron Burr and George Clinton…Election of 1800 was only Presidential election to end in a tie … Jefferson and Burr each got 73 electoral votes and John Adams had 65…Under rules at that time, the House of Representatives then voted, and made Jefferson President and Burr Vice President…Jefferson was the person who wrote the Declaration of Independence, when he was just 33 years old…Achieved fame as a diplomat, political thinker, architect, inventor and founder of the University of Virginia…Greatly expanded U.S. territory with Louisiana Purchase from France.

James Madison
4th President

President, March 4, 1809 to March 3, 1817...Took office at age 57, left at 65...College: Princeton...Party: Democratic-Republican...VPs: George Clinton and Elbridge Gerry...Smallest President, he weighed less than 100 pounds and stood 5-4...First President to wear modern trousers (previous Presidents wore breeches or knickers with silk stockings)...Madison was the only President to lead troops in battle while in office when he took command of forces fighting to protect Washington, D.C. during the War of 1812...His wife was the flamboyant Dolley Madison who dazzled the nation with her spectacular parties and stylish clothes...At one of her many dinner parties, she introduced ice cream to America.

James Monroe
5th President

President, March 4, 1817 to March 3, 1825...Took office at age 58, left at 66...College: William & Mary...Party: Democratic-Republican...VP: Daniel Tompkins...Was so popular, in what was called "the era of good feeling," no one ran against him for his second-term election...Only President to have a foreign capital named for him. Helped Liberia become an independent nation, and they named their capital Monrovia...Despite his great ability and intelligence, he left office in financial distress and had to move in with his daughter and son-in-law...Died broke...His death on July 4, 1831 completed amazing coincidence of three of first five Presidents all dying on July 4. John Adams and Thomas Jefferson had both died on July 4, 1826.

John Quincy Adams
6th President

President, March 4, 1825 to March 3, 1829... Took office at age 57, left at 61...College: Harvard...Party: Democratic-Republican...VP: John Calhoun...First person to become President whose father was also President...Lost popular vote, but won Presidency in Electoral College...Four of first six Presidents, oddly, all took office at age 57, but none has done so since John Quincy...Was famous for swimming in the nude in Potomac River...Only President to die on floor of Congress...After leaving Presidency, he was elected to House of Representatives nine times. During his last term, he suffered a stroke while sitting at his House desk. He died in the House chamber.

Andrew Jackson
7th President

President from March 4, 1829 to March 3, 1837…Took office at age 61, left at 69…College: None…Party: Democratic-Republican…VPs: John   Calhoun   and   Martin   Van   Buren…All previous Presidents had come from wealthy families, but Jackson was the first "common man" to be President…Was born in a log cabin to poor Scottish-Irish   immigrants…Orphaned   at 14…Became famous military man, winning the Battle of New Orleans in the War of 1812…Had controversial marriage, marrying a woman who thought she was divorced.   It turned out the divorce   wasn't   final.   Jackson's   political opponents dogged him on issue for the rest of his career and Jackson fought a pistol duel against a man who insulted Jackson's wife. Jackson killed his opponent… Most likely, could have won a third term, but following precedent set by George Washington, he refused to run for more than two terms. (There was no law at the time prohibiting third terms.)

Martin Van Buren
8th President

President, March 4, 1837 to March 3, 1841...Took office at age 54, left at 58...College: None...Party: Democratic-Republican...VP: Richard Johnson...The word OK came into our language because of Van Buren...He was from the town of Old Kinderhook, New York...His supporters took the initials of the town and formed the OK Club. They said Van Buren was OK— equating it to good or all right...Gradually people everywhere started using OK for anything that was all right, and a new word was born...Although Van Buren was popular when elected, he quickly lost favor during the financial panic of 1837 and was soundly beaten for a second term...When he presided over Senate as VP under Jackson, there were threats against his life, and he often put two pistols in front of him on his desk...Married his cousin, Hannah Hoes.

William Henry Harrison
9th President

President, March 4, 1841 to April 4, 1841...Took office at age 68, left at 68...College: Hampden-Sydney...Party: Whig...VP: John Tyler...Only President who never signed a bill or performed any significant Presidential action... He caught a cold at his inauguration on March 4 and died of pneumonia 31 days later...Spent much of his short term in bed...When he ran for President he used one of the most famous campaign slogans of all time—"Tippecanoe and Tyler, too"...He had become a hero leading U.S. troops to victory in the Battle of Tippecanoe, and his VP was Tyler...His son John became the only man to be the son and father of a President...John's son (and William's grandson) was Benjamin Harrison, the 23rd President.

John Tyler
10th President

President, April 6, 1841 to March 3, 1845...Took office at age 51, left at 55...College: William & Mary...Party: Whig...VP: None...The U.S. had three different Presidents in just over one month in 1841...Van Buren left office March 3, was succeeded by Harrison who died April 4, and Tyler took office April 6...His Presidency wasn't particularly memorable, but he did set a record...He had 15 children, more than any other President—and he had two sons named John and two named Robert...By his first wife he had eight children, including Robert and John...By his second wife he had seven children including another Robert and John...The first Robert and John were still living when the second Robert and John were born...Tyler was the only President whose death was officially ignored...The Civil War was on when he died and since Tyler lived in the South, the government took no notice of his death...No flags at half-staff, no announcement, no proclamation.

James Polk
11th President

President, March 4, 1845 to March 3, 1849...Took office at age 49, left at 53...College: University of North Carolina...Party: Democrat...VP: George Dallas...That Polk became President was a surprise to him and the nation...He wasn't even a candidate, but a deadlocked nominating convention finally turned to him...In the election, he was a heavy underdog to the better-known Henry Clay...But Polk beat Clay in one of the biggest upsets in Presidential history...Polk said he disliked being President and announced early in his term that he wouldn't run for a second term...He couldn't wait for retirement, but died just 103 days after leaving office...His wife Sarah banned dancing and alcoholic beverages from the White House.

Zachary Taylor
12th President

President, March 4, 1849 to July 9, 1850...Took office at age 65, left at 66...College: None...Party: Whig...VP: Millard Fillmore... Taylor was a career army officer and was the first President who had not been a member of the Continental Congress or the U.S. Congress...Was Mexican War hero...Didn't know he was nominated for President...He was at an army post when a letter came informing him of his nomination...He refused the letter because it came postage-due...Finally, a messenger was sent to tell him of his nomination...Called "Old Rough and Ready"...His son-in-law was Jefferson Davis who would become president of the Confederacy in 1861.

Millard Fillmore
13th President

President, July 10, 1850 to March 3, 1853...Took office at age 50, left at 53...College: None...Party: Whig...VP: None...Fillmore was the last President to be neither a Democrat or a Republican...He was born in a log cabin in upstate New York...Left school early to help support his family, and could barely read as a teenager...Was determined to become educated and began intensive self-study...By the time he was 46, he was appointed chancellor of the University of Buffalo, and by 50 was President of the United States...Was not a popular President, and his and his party's political career ended after his first term.

Franklin Pierce
14th President

President, March 4, 1853 to March 3, 1857...Took office at age 48, left at 52...College: Bowdoin...Party: Democrat...VP: William King...In his small college class were two men who, like Pierce, would achieve national fame— authors-to-be Nathaniel Hawthorne and Henry Wadsworth Longfellow...Personal tragedies dogged Pierce and his wife, Jane...Their 12-year-old son was killed in a railroad accident less than two months before Pierce was inaugurated...Their first child had died as an infant and their other child had died at age 4...Because of her grief, Mrs. Pierce had no interest in serving as First Lady and always dressed in black...Pierce's Vice President, William King, died one month after taking office...Illness prevented King from coming to Washington, and he was never in the capital during his brief term...To compound his unhappy Presidency, Pierce failed to get his party's nomination for a second term.

James Buchanan
15th President

President, March 4, 1857 to March 3, 1861...Took office at age 65, left at 69...College: Dickinson...Party: Democrat...VP: John Breckinridge...Buchanan was the only President who never married...His niece, Harriet Lane, served as White House hostess during his term...Buchanan's VP, John Breckinridge, was the youngest Vice President in U.S. history, inaugurated at age 36, and would have been the only President in his 30s had anything happened to Buchanan...The approaching Civil War clouded Buchanan's Presidency and he left office blamed by many for indecisiveness.

Abraham Lincoln
16th President

President, March 4, 1861 to April 15, 1865...Took office at age 52, left at 56...College: None...Party: Republican...VPs: Hannibal Hamlin and Andrew Johnson...Lincoln was the tallest President, standing 6-4...Was the first President to wear a beard in office...A prominent actor, Edwin Booth, saved Lincoln's son, Robert, from death by pulling him from train tracks after the boy had fallen off a platform—but it was Booth's brother, John Wilkes Booth who would later assassinate Lincoln...One month after Lincoln took office, the Civil War began, and 6 days before his death, the war ended...Remembered for his eloquence in debates with Stephen Douglas, the Emancipation Proclamation and the Gettysburg Address...His wife, Mary, never called him by his first name...She always referred to him as "Mr. Lincoln."

Andrew Johnson
17th President

President, April 15, 1865 to March 3, 1869...Took office at age 56, left at 60...College: None...Party: Democrat...VP: None...Never attended school and couldn't read or write until taught by his future wife, Eliza, at age 17...Johnson married her when he was 18, she 16...At age 22, he was elected mayor of Greenville, Tennessee, and later was elected to the state assembly, the U.S. House and Senate and governor of Tennessee...Although a Democrat, he was selected by the Republican, Lincoln, for Vice President in attempt to please Southern Democrats...He was the first President to be impeached...He was charged with removing a cabinet member in defiance of a Congressional act, although the real reason was disagreements over Reconstruction...Johnson was acquitted by the margin of one vote and continued to serve out his term.

Ulysses Grant
18th President

President, March 4, 1869 to March 3, 1877…Took office at age 46, left at 54…College: U.S. Military Academy…Party: Republican… VPs: Schuyler Colfax and Henry Wilson…Early in his adult life, Grant failed in several businesses and was then discharged from the Army for alcoholism…But he got his life together, reentered the Army and went on to a successful military and political career…Grant was the first President to run against a woman…Victoria Woodhull had been nominated for President on a 3rd-party Equal Rights ticket, but Grant won over her and his Democratic opponent, Horace Greeley…The term "lobbyists" came into the language during Grant's Presidency…He would relax most evenings in the lobby of the Willard Hotel in Washington, enjoying an after-dinner cigar…Those seeking favors would approach him there—and he coined the name "lobbyists" for them…A favorite old quiz question is, "Who's buried in Grant's Tomb?"…Most people say Grant—but that's only half right…His wife Julia is also buried there.

Rutherford Hayes
19th President

President, March 4, 1877 to March 3, 1881...Took office at age 54, left at 58...College: Kenyon...Party: Republican...VP: William Wheeler...Hayes was the only man elected President by one vote...In his election, neither he or his opponent, Samuel Tilden, had the necessary Electoral votes...The election was thrown into Congress where a 15-man commission was picked to choose the winner...Hayes won 8-7 and became President...For all the trouble he had getting elected, Hayes didn't like the job...He announced early in his term that he wouldn't run again, and he stuck to that...His wife Lucy mandated that no alcohol be allowed in the White House; she always served lemonade—and became known throughout the country as "Lemonade Lucy."

101

James Garfield
20th President

President, March 4, 1881 to Sept. 19, 1881…Took office at age 49, left at 49…College: Williams…Party: Republican…VP: Chester Arthur…Garfield completed an unusual streak of three consecutive Presidents all being former Army generals and all being from Ohio—Grant, Hayes and Garfield…Garfield had the second-shortest Presidency…Less than 4 months after taking office, he was shot at the Washington railroad station by a disappointed office-seeker, Charles Guiteau…80 days later Garfield died from the wounds…The only shorter Presidency was William Henry Harrison's 31 days…Garfield's Secretary of War was Abraham Lincoln's son Robert—and it was Robert who was on the scene for three Presidential assassinations… Robert was with his father after Abraham Lincoln was shot, then was with Garfield at the railroad station, and would be with McKinley 20 years later when that President was shot.

Chester Arthur
21st President

President, Sept. 20, 1881 to March 3, 1885...Took office at age 50, left at 54...College: Union...Party: Republican...VP: None...Arthur was the only President who had never been a member of Congress, a governor of a state, a famous Army general or had held a high-level government job...He had been a lawyer and the Collector for the Port of New York—and was fired from that job...He had dabbled in politics, became a delegate to the Republican convention and was nominated as Vice President as a compromise candidate in a surprise move...Despite his lack of experience when he took over the Presidency on Garfield's death, Arthur turned out to be a fairly effective President, although he was not nominated to run for a second term.

Grover Cleveland
22nd & 24th President

President, March 4, 1885 to March 3, 1889 and from March 4, 1893 to March 3, 1897...Took office at age 47, left at 59...College: None...Party: Democrat...VPs: Thomas Hendricks and Adlai Stevenson (grandfather of future Presidential candidate)...Cleveland was the only President to serve two non-consecutive terms...He was defeated for reelection in 1888, but ran again in 1892 and won...He was the only county sheriff to become President, and as sheriff in Buffalo hanged two men, personally pulling the lever that caused the hangings...Cleveland was a bachelor when he first came to the White House, but then married 21-year-old Frances Folsom... Ms. Folsom became the youngest First Lady in history...They had a daughter, Ruth, who inspired the name for a candy bar...Ruth was often seen playing with Cleveland at the White House and she captivated the nation...She was called Baby Ruth—and the candy bar was named for her—and not the baseball player, Babe Ruth, as is popularly believed.

Benjamin Harrison
23rd President

President, March 4, 1889 to March 3, 1893...Took office at age 55, left at 59...College: Miami of Ohio...Party: Republican...VP: Levi Morton...Harrison is the only grandson of a former President to attain the Presidency himself...His grandfather was William Henry Harrison, the 9th President...In his election for President, Benjamin Harrison got fewer popular votes than Grover Cleveland, but beat him in the Electoral College...The highlight of Harrison's rather quiet term was the passage of the Sherman Antitrust Act...Harrison's wife was ill and became an invalid during part of his term...His wife's niece, Mary, was brought to the White House to become hostess—and after his wife died, the 65-year-old Harrison married 37-year-old Mary...They had a daughter, giving Harrison a child who was younger than his four grandchildren.

William McKinley
25th President

President, March 4, 1897 to Sept. 14, 1901...Took office at age 54, left at 58...College: Allegheny...Party: Republican...VPs: Garret Hobart and Theodore Roosevelt...Early in McKinley's first term, the U.S. battleship Maine was blown up in Havana harbor, and the Spanish-American War was on...In the war, the U.S. became a world power, driving the Spanish out of the Western Hemisphere and acquiring Puerto Rico, the Philippines, Samoa and Guam... McKinley's future Vice President Theodore Roosevelt became a hero leading the "Rough Riders" with the famous San Juan charge...McKinley was the third President to be assassinated...He was shot by an anarchist, Leon Czolosz, at a business exposition in Buffalo.

Theodore Roosevelt
26th President

President, Sept. 14, 1901 to March 3, 1909...Took office at age 42, left at 49...College: Harvard...Party: Republican...VP: Charles Fairbanks...Roosevelt was the youngest U.S. President, taking office at 42...Sickly as a child, he was determined to live a vigorous life...He took up swimming, hiking, hunting, horseback riding and boxing...Had three careers before becoming President...He was a politician, serving in the New York state assembly and as governor of New York...He was a rancher, running two ranches in 14-and-16-hour days, and he was a military man...Had one spectacular failure, losing an election for mayor of New York City—and going down in history as the only person to lose a mayoral race and win a Presidential election...He was shot in the chest during a campaign speech, but was determined to finish the speech, and survived...Actively fought corruption in politics and big business...Teddy bears were named for him.

William Howard Taft
27th President

President, March 4, 1909 to March 3, 1913...Took office at age 51, left at 55...College: Yale...Party: Republican...VP: James Sherman... Taft is the only person who served as both President of the United States and Chief Justice of the U.S. Supreme Court...Last President to wear a mustache in office...Heaviest, by far, of any President, weighing over 300 pounds...Drafted amendment that made income tax legal... Vigorously continued Roosevelt's trust-busting policies...But Roosevelt, who endorsed Taft for Presidency in 1908, became disenchanted with him and ran against him on a 3rd party ticket in 1912...That effectively defeated Taft's reelection bid and gave election to Woodrow Wilson...Taft's son Robert tried for the Presidency in the 1940s and 50s, but failed to get nomination.

Woodrow Wilson
28th President

President, March 4, 1913 to March 3, 1921...Took office at age 56, left at 64...College: Princeton...Party: Democrat...VP: Thomas Marshall...Wilson was the most educated President, having earned a doctoral degree...His Ph.D. was in political science...Before becoming U.S. President, he was president of Princeton University and had taught at Bryn Mawr, Wesleyan and Princeton...Was also governor of New Jersey...Led U.S. in World War I...Toward the end of his second term, he suffered a stroke while touring the nation to get support for his peace plans...Was a virtual invalid for months... During this time, his wife Edith, in effect, functioned as President—making her the first woman President in all but name and official designation.

Warren Harding
29th President

President, March 4, 1921 to August 2, 1923...Took office at age 55, left at 57...College: Ohio Central...Party: Republican...VP: Calvin Coolidge...Harding's election theme was a "Return to Normalcy" after World War I, and the U.S., ready for the Jazz Age and prosperity, overwhelmingly elected him...The night he won the election, Nov. 2, 1920, marked the first time election returns were broadcast...Radio station KDKA, Pittsburgh, went on the air as the first commercial station...The first election night announcer was Leo Rosenberg...Scandal soon touched Harding's administration and as rumors began to circulate, Harding became ill and died a little more than two years after taking office.

Calvin Coolidge
30th President

President, August 3, 1923 to March 3, 1929...Took office at 51, left at 57...College: Amherst...Party: Republican...VP: Charles Dawes...Coolidge was the only President born on the 4th of July, and the only President sworn in by his father...Coolidge was at his home in Vermont when word came late at night that President Harding had died...Coolidge was awakened and given the oath of office by his father who was a justice of the peace...Reports said Coolidge's first act as President was to go back to sleep, and he slept soundly, they say...He was a quiet, reserved man, and when he ran for another term, in 1924, his slogan was "Keep Cool with Coolidge"... Coolidge presided over one of the great economic booms in history, saying "the business of America is business"...He probably could have been elected for another term in 1928, but famously said, "I do not choose to run."

Herbert Hoover
31st President

President, March 4, 1929 to March 3, 1933...Took office at 54, left at 58...College: Stanford...Party: Republican...VP: Charles Curtis... Hoover was the first President born west of the Mississippi...He was born in West Branch, Iowa...Hoover easily won the Presidency, beating his opponent, Al Smith, with 84 percent of the Electoral vote...But he became President at the wrong time...A little more than seven months after taking office, the stock market crashed and the economy collapsed, ushering in the Great Depression...Hoover was considered a bright, decent man, but was criticized for not doing enough to help the nation's financial woes, and when he ran for a second term, he was crushed by Franklin Roosevelt who got 90 percent of the Electoral vote...Hoover was personally wealthy and refused to take any salary as President...After leaving office, he always donated his government pension to charity.

Franklin Roosevelt
32nd President

President, March 4, 1933 to April 12, 1945...Took office at age 51, left at 63...College: Harvard...Party: Democrat...VPs: John Garner, Henry Wallace and Harry Truman...Longest-serving President in history...Elected to four terms, now prohibited by law...Adept at inspiring the nation through the Great Depression and then World War II...Reached the people with his famous "fireside chats"...Those speeches were made while Roosevelt was seated, ironically, beside the only fireplace in the White House that didn't work...Overcame physical disability...An attack of polio in 1921 left him unable to stand or walk unaided the rest of his life...His memorable quotes included a "New Deal for the American people," "The only thing we have to fear is fear itself," and "Yesterday, December 7, was a date that will live in infamy."...He died of a cerebral hemorrhage less than two months into his 4th term...His wife Eleanor, a distant cousin, became a public figure herself and was a U.S. delegate to the UN.

Harry Truman
33rd President

President, April 12, 1945 to Jan. 20, 1953...Took office at age 60, left at 68...College: None...Party: Democrat...VP: Alben Barkley... Truman was the last President to have never attended college...Seemed overwhelmed when, as Vice President, he had to replace Roosevelt as President...He said he felt as if the stars, the sun and the moon had just fallen on him...But he grew in the job, and when he ran for President in his own right in 1948, he scored the biggest upset victory in Presidential history...Virtually every poll pointed to a sure win for Thomas Dewey...Life magazine titled a picture of Dewey before the election as "The next President"...The Chicago Tribune ran their infamous headline, "Dewey defeats Truman" in their early editions election night...The election wasn't close...Truman won the Electoral College vote by 303 to 189.

Dwight Eisenhower
34th President

President, Jan. 20, 1953 to Jan. 19, 1961... Took office at age 62, left at 70...College: U.S. Military Academy...Party: Republican...VP: Richard Nixon...Eisenhower ran for only two political offices in his life, and won the Presidency both times...Was the last of 12 Army generals to become President...First President to have played college football...But his football career at Army ended when he tried to tackle Hall of Famer Jim Thorpe...Ike broke his leg and never played again...Was an obscure Army colonel when he was promoted to general over more senior officers, and eventually led Allied forces on D-Day...Easily won his two Presidential elections over Adlai Stevenson, both times...Proposed the Interstate Highway System, with the main motivation being to provide good, super highways for rapid troop and supply movement in case of war...Unknown to many, the official name of the Interstates is the Dwight D. Eisenhower Interstate System.

John Kennedy
35th President

President, Jan. 20, 1961 to Nov. 22, 1963...Took office at age 43, left at 45...College: Harvard...Party: Democrat...VP: Lyndon Johnson... Kennedy is the first, and only, non-Protestant to be U.S. President...He was Catholic...At 43, he was second-youngest President...Only Theodore Roosevelt, at 42, was younger...Was fourth President to be assassinated, and there were amazing similarities between his and Lincoln's assassinations...Both were shot on a Friday, seated next to their wives...Their assassins' names both had 15 letters—John Wilkes Booth and Lee Harvey Oswald...Booth had been born in 1839, Oswald in 1939...Lincoln was elected in 1860, Kennedy in 1960...Both were succeeded by men named Johnson—Andrew Johnson born in 1808 and Lyndon Johnson born in 1908...Lincoln's secretary was named Kennedy and Kennedy's secretary was named Lincoln...The car in which Kennedy was riding when he was shot was...a Lincoln.

Lyndon Johnson
36th President

President, Nov. 22, 1963 to Jan. 20, 1969...Took office at age 55, left at 60...College: Southwest Texas...Party: Democrat...VP: Hubert Humphrey...Johnson was the only President to be sworn in by a woman...As he was leaving Dallas for Washington after John Kennedy was shot, Texas judge Sarah Hughes swore Johnson in as President aboard Air Force One at Love Field in Dallas as Mrs. Kennedy looked on...Was once a school teacher...Won passage of many "Great Society" programs with civil rights, anti-poverty, aid-to education and health care (Medicare and Medicaid) legislation...The initials LBJ applied to himself (Lyndon Baines Johnson), his wife (Lady Bird Johnson) and their two daughters (Lynda Bird Johnson and Luci Baines Johnson), and even one of their dogs (Little Beagle Johnson).

117

Richard Nixon
37th President

President, Jan. 20, 1969 to August 9, 1974...Took office at age 56, left at 61...College: Whittier...Party: Republican...VPs: Spiro Agnew and Gerald Ford...Nixon was the first and only President to resign from office, during the Watergate case...Lost close Presidential election to John Kennedy in 1960, then lost race for governor of California in 1962, but came back to win Presidency in 1968 and won a second term in 1972 by big margin...Only person besides Franklin Roosevelt to be elected to the Vice Presidency or Presidency four times; he had won two Vice-Presidential elections under Eisenhower and two Presidential elections in his own right...Second President to have played college football...He played for Whittier in the 1930s...His wife Pat had been a movie actress who appeared in the first Technicolor film, "Trail of the Lonesome Pine"...Their daughter Julie married the grandson of President Eisenhower, David Eisenhower, for whom Camp David was named.

Gerald Ford
38th President

President, August 9, 1974 to Jan. 19, 1977...Took office at age 61, left at 64...College: Michigan...Party: Republican...VP: Nelson Rockefeller...Ford was the only President who was never elected either President or Vice President in a national election...He was named Vice President under the 25th Amendment when Spiro Agnew resigned and then succeeded to the Presidency when Nixon resigned...His original name was Leslie King...His mother divorced his father whose last name was King, and then married Gerald Ford who adopted the future President and renamed him Gerald Ford Jr....Ford played on national championship college football teams at Michigan in 1932 and 1933 as a center, and was voted Most Valuable Player on the 1934 team...He was an assistant football coach at Yale from 1935 to 1940...His wife Betty had been a professional dancer with the Martha Graham Dance Company...His pardoning of Richard Nixon might have been a major cause of his unsuccessful reelection bid.

Jimmy Carter
39th President

President, Jan. 20, 1977 to Jan. 19, 1981...Took office at age 52, left at 56...College: U.S. Naval Academy...Party: Democrat...VP: Walter Mondale...Carter was the first President to officially go by his nickname...Some other Presidents had nicknames, like Teddy Roosevelt—but they were never referred to that way in any kind of formal setting...James Carter always insisted on being called Jimmy...Carter left his naval career to run the family peanut farm in Plains, Georgia, after his father's death...First President from the Deep South since before the Civil War...Was a likeable man, but his one term was dogged by the Iran hostage crisis and a weak economy...Amazingly, was first President born in a hospital...All previous Presidents were born at home, the custom well into the 20th century...Ran for a second term, but was soundly defeated by Ronald Reagan.

Ronald Reagan
40th President

President, Jan. 20, 1981 to Jan. 19, 1989...Took office at age 69, left at 77...College: Eureka...Party: Republican...VP: George Bush... Reagan was the oldest man ever to be President...Aside from Reagan the only other 70-year-old President was Eisenhower who left office at that age, while Reagan left at 77...Reagan was the only divorced President...He divorced actress Jane Wyman the year she won an Academy Award for "Johnny Belinda," in 1949...He then married another actress, Nancy Davis and they appeared in one movie together, "Hell Cats of the Navy"...In all, Reagan acted in over 50 films, including "Knute Rockne—All American," in which he played running back George Gipp, and reenacted the famous "Win one for the Gipper" speech...Was a popular President and effective communicator who won landslide victories in his two Presidential elections.

George Bush
41st President

President, Jan. 20, 1989 to Jan. 19, 1993...Took office at age 64, left at 68...College: Yale...Party: Republican...VP: Dan Quayle... Bush was the first President named George since Washington...Bush and his family held more high offices than any other family in U.S. history...His father was a U.S. Senator...He was a U.S. Congressman, an ambassador, head of the CIA, Vice President and President...One of his sons became a governor and then President, and another son a governor...Bush held one of the highest Presidential approval ratings of all time during and after the Gulf War, but lost popularity during a recession shortly afterward and was defeated in a reelection try.

Bill Clinton
42nd President

President, Jan. 20, 1993 to Jan. 19, 2001...Took office at age 46, left at 54...College: Georgetown...Party: Democrat...VP: Al Gore... Clinton was born with the name Bill Blythe, and had that name for 16 years...His father, whose last name was Blythe, was killed in an automobile accident, and his mother later married a man named Clinton...When the future President was a teenager, he changed his name to Bill Clinton...Became a Rhodes Scholar...One of only 12 (of 42) Presidents to serve two full terms...He was the second President impeached, and like the first, Andrew Johnson, he was acquitted and continued to serve...His wife Hillary became the first First Lady to be elected to Congress, serving in the U.S. Senate.

George W. Bush
43rd President

President, Jan. 20, 2001...Took office at age 54...College: Yale...VP: Dick Cheney...Bush was the fourth President to lose a popular vote and yet win the election with Electoral votes...The others were John Quincy Adams, Rutherford Hayes and Benjamin Harrison...Another similarity with John Quincy Adams is that they are the only two Presidents whose fathers were also President...Although Bush is thought of as a Texan, he was not born in Texas...Was born in New Haven, Connecticut on July 6, 1946...Surprisingly, in U.S. history, only four Presidents had fathers alive when they became President...The other three besides George W. Bush were John Kennedy, Calvin Coolidge and John Quincy Adams...What does the "W" stand for in Bush's name?...His full name is George Walker Bush—but his father also has a "W" for an initial...The first Bush was George Herbert Walker Bush...Walker comes from the first President Bush's mother whose maiden name was Dorothy Walker.

SIX

The Fifty States
and the District of Columbia

Six

THE 50 STATES

Alabama

- Capital - Montgomery

- Nickname - Camellia or Yellowhammer State

- Entered Union - 1819

- Joined as 22nd state

- Biggest city - Birmingham

- Central Time Zone

- Named after the Alabamas Indian tribe.

Alaska

- Capital – Juneau

- Nickname - The Last Frontier

- Entered Union - 1959

- Joined as 49th state

- Biggest city - Anchorage

- Alaska and Hawaii-Aleutian Time Zones

- Named after Eskimo word for "Great Lands."

Arizona

- Capital – Phoenix

- Nickname - Grand Canyon State

- Entered union - 1912

- Joined as 48th state

- Biggest city - Phoenix

- Mountain Time Zone

- Named after Indian word for "Silver-Bearing."

Arkansas

- Capital - Little Rock

- Nickname - Razorback or Natural State

- Entered Union - 1836

- Joined as 25th state

- Biggest city – Little Rock

- Central Time Zone

- Named after Indian word for "South Wind."

California

- Capital – Sacramento

- Nickname - Golden State

- Entered Union - 1850

- Joined as 31st state

- Biggest city – Los Angeles

- Pacific Time Zone

- Named after an imaginary paradise in a Spanish novel.

Colorado

- Capital – Denver

- Nickname - Centennial State

- Entered Union - 1876

- Joined as 38th state

- Biggest city - Denver

- Mountain Time Zone

- Named after a Spanish word for "red."

Connecticut

- Capital – Hartford

- Nickname – Constitution or Nutmeg State

- Entered Union - 1788

- Joined as 5th state

- Biggest city - Bridgeport

- Eastern Time Zone

- Named after an Indian word for "Long River."

Delaware

- Capital – Dover

- Nickname - First or Diamond State

- Entered Union - 1787

- Joined as 1st state

- Biggest city - Wilmington

- Eastern Time Zone

- Named for Lord De La Warr.

Florida

- Capital – Tallahassee

- Nickname - Sunshine State

- Entered Union - 1845

- Joined as 27th state

- Biggest city - Jacksonville

- Eastern and Central Time Zones

- Named after Spanish word for "Flowery."

Georgia

- Capital – Atlanta

- Nickname - Peach State

- Entered Union - 1788

- Joined as 4th state

- Biggest city - Atlanta

- Eastern Time Zone

- Named for King George II of England.

Hawaii

- Capital – Honolulu

- Nickname - Aloha State

- Entered Union - 1959

- Joined as 50th state

- Biggest city – Honolulu

- Hawaii-Aleutian Time Zone

- Named after Polynesian word for "Homeland."

Idaho

- Capital – Boise

- Nickname - Gem State

- Entered Union - 1890

- Joined as 43rd state

- Biggest city - Boise

- Mountain and Pacific Time Zones

- Name origin - Unknown.

Illinois

- Capital – Springfield

- Nickname – Land of Lincoln or Prairie State

- Entered Union - 1818

- Joined as 21st state

- Biggest city - Chicago

- Central Time Zone

- Named after Indian word for "Warriors."

Indiana

- Capital – Indianapolis

- Nickname - Hoosier State

- Entered Union - 1816

- Joined as 19th state

- Biggest city - Indianapolis

- Eastern and Central Time Zones

- Named after Land of Indians.

Iowa

- Capital - Des Moines

- Nickname - Hawkeye State

- Entered Union - 1846

- Joined as 29th state

- Biggest city – Des Moines

- Central Time Zone

- Named after Indian word for "Beautiful Land."

Kansas

- Capital – Topeka

- Nickname - Sunflower State

- Entered Union - 1861

- Joined as 34th state

- Biggest city - Wichita

- Central and Mountain Time Zones

- Named after Indian word for "South Wind."

Kentucky

- Capital – Frankfort

- Nickname - Bluegrass State

- Entered Union - 1792

- Joined as 15th state

- Biggest city - Louisville

- Eastern and Central Time Zones

- Named after Indian word for "Meadowland People."

Louisiana

- Capital - Baton Rouge

- Nickname - Pelican State

- Entered Union - 1812

- Joined as 18th state

- Biggest city – New Orleans

- Central Time Zone

- Named for King Louis XIV of France.

Maine

- Capital – Augusta

- Nickname - Pine Tree State

- Entered Union - 1820

- Joined as 23rd state

- Biggest City - Portland

- Eastern Time Zone

- Named for Ancient French province.

Maryland

- Capital – Annapolis

- Nickname - Old Line State

- Entered Union - 1788

- Joined as 7th state

- Biggest city - Baltimore

- Eastern Time Zone

- Named for Queen Maria of England.

Massachusetts

- Capital – Boston

- Nickname - Bay State

- Entered Union - 1788

- Joined as 6th state

- Biggest city - Boston

- Eastern Time Zone

- Named after Indian word for "Large Hill."

Michigan

- Capital – Lansing

- Nickname - Wolverine or Great Lakes State

- Entered Union - 1837

- Joined as 26th state

- Biggest city - Detroit

- Eastern Time Zone

- Named after Indian word for "Great Water."

Minnesota

- Capital - St. Paul

- Nickname - Gopher or North Star State

- Entered Union - 1858

- Joined as 32nd state

- Biggest city – Minneapolis

- Central Time Zone

- Named after Indian word for "Sky-Tinted Water."

Mississippi

- Capital – Jackson

- Nickname - Magnolia State

- Entered Union - 1817

- Joined as 20th state

- Biggest city - Jackson

- Central Time Zone

- Named after Indian word for "Gathering of Waters."

Missouri

- Capital - Jefferson City

- Nickname - Show Me State

- Entered Union – 1821

- Joined as 24th state

- Biggest city – Kansas City

- Central Time Zone

- Named after Indian word for "River of Big Canoes."

Montana

- Capital – Helena

- Nickname - Treasure State

- Entered Union - 1889

- Joined as 41st state

- Biggest city - Billings

- Mountain Time Zone

- Named after the Spanish word for "Mountainous."

Nebraska

- Capital – Lincoln

- Nickname - Cornhusker State

- Entered Union - 1867

- Joined as 37th state

- Biggest city - Omaha

- Central and Mountain Time Zones

- Named after Indian word for "Broad River."

Nevada

- Capital - Carson City

- Nickname - Silver State

- Entered Union - 1864

- Joined as 36th state

- Biggest city – Las Vegas

- Pacific Time Zone

- Named after Spanish word for "Snow Clad."

New Hampshire

- Capital – Concord

- Nickname - Granite State

- Entered Union - 1788

- Joined as 9th state

- Biggest city - Manchester

- Eastern Time Zone

- Named for county in England.

New Jersey

- Capital – Trenton

- Nickname - Garden State

- Entered Union - 1787

- Joined as 3rd state

- Biggest city - Newark

- Eastern Time Zone

- Named for England's Isle of Jersey.

New Mexico

- Capital - Santa Fe

- Nickname - Land of Enchantment

- Entered Union - 1912

- Joined as 47th state

- Biggest city - Albuquerque

- Mountain Time Zone

- Named by Spaniards in Mexico.

The States

New York

- Capital - Albany

- Nickname - Empire State

- Entered Union - 1788

- Joined as 11th state

- Biggest city – New York

- Eastern Time Zone

- Named for Duke of York of England.

North Carolina

- Capital – Raleigh

- Nickname - Tar Heel State

- Entered Union - 1789

- Joined as 12th state

- Biggest city - Charlotte

- Eastern Time Zone

- Named from Latin name for King Charles I of England.

North Dakota

- Capital – Bismarck

- Nickname - Peace Garden State

- Entered Union - 1889

- Joined as 39th state

- Biggest city - Fargo

- Central and Mountain Time Zones

- Named after Indian word for "Friend."

Ohio

- Capital – Columbus

- Nickname - Buckeye State

- Entered Union - 1803

- Joined as 17th state

- Biggest city - Columbus

- Eastern Time Zone

- Named after Indian word for "Good River."

Oklahoma

- Capital - Oklahoma City

- Nickname - Sooner State

- Entered Union - 1907

- Joined as 46th state

- Biggest city – Oklahoma City

- Central Time Zone

- Named after Indian word for "Red Man."

Oregon

- Capital – Salem

- Nickname - Beaver State

- Entered Union - 1859

- Joined as 33rd state

- Biggest city - Portland

- Pacific and Mountain Time Zones

- Name Origin - Unknown.

Pennsylvania

- Capital – Harrisburg

- Nickname - Keystone State

- Entered Union - 1787

- Joined as 2nd state

- Biggest city - Philadelphia

- Eastern Time Zone

- Named for William Penn. Sylvania came from woodland.

Rhode Island

- Capital – Providence

- Nickname - Ocean State

- Entered Union - 1790

- Joined as 13th state

- Biggest city - Providence

- Eastern Time Zone

- Named for Isle of Rhodes in Mediterranean

South Carolina

- Capital – Columbia

- Nickname - Palmetto State

- Entered Union - 1788

- Joined as 8th state

- Biggest city - Columbia

- Eastern Time Zone

- Named from Latin name for King Charles I of England.

South Dakota

- Capital – Pierre

- Nickname – Mt. Rushmore State

- Entered Union - 1889

- Joined as 40th state

- Biggest city – Sioux Falls

- Central and Mountain Time Zones

- Named after Indian word for "Friend."

Tennessee

- Capital – Nashville

- Nickname - Volunteer State

- Entered Union - 1796

- Joined as 16th state

- Biggest city - Memphis

- Eastern and Central Time Zones

- Named after Indian name for "Villages."

Texas

- Capital – Austin

- Nickname - Lone Star State

- Entered Union - 1845

- Joined as 28th state

- Biggest city - Houston

- Central and Mountain Time Zones

- Named after Indian word for "Ally."

Utah

- Capital - Salt Lake City

- Nickname - Beehive State

- Entered Union - 1896

- Joined as 45th state

- Biggest city – Salt Lake City

- Mountain Time Zone

- Named for Ute Indian Tribe.

Vermont

- Capital – Montpelier

- Nickname - Green Mountain State

- Entered Union - 1791

- Joined as 14th state

- Biggest city - Burlington

- Eastern Time Zone

- Named from French words for "Green Mountain."

Virginia

- Capital – Richmond

- Nickname - Old Dominion

- Entered Union - 1788

- Joined as 10th state

- Biggest city – Virginia Beach

- Eastern Time Zone

- Named for Queen Elizabeth I, Virgin Queen of England.

Washington

- Capital – Olympia

- Nickname - Evergreen State

- Entered Union - 1889

- Joined as 42nd state

- Biggest city - Seattle

- Pacific Time Zone

- Named for George Washington.

West Virginia

- Capital – Charleston

- Nickname - Mountain State

- Entered Union - 1863

- Joined as 35th state

- Biggest city - Charleston

- Eastern Time Zone

- Named for Queen Elizabeth I, Virgin Queen of England.

Wisconsin

- Capital – Madison

- Nickname - Badger State

- Entered Union - 1848

- Joined as 30th state

- Biggest city - Milwaukee

- Central Time Zone

- Named after Indian word for "Grassy Place."

Wyoming

- Capital – Cheyenne

- Nickname - Cowboy or Equality State

- Entered Union - 1890

- Joined as 44th state

- Biggest city - Cheyenne

- Mountain Time Zone

- Named after Indian word for "Large Plain."

WASHINGTON, D.C.

Why Washington became the U.S. capital

Surprisingly, between 1776 and 1800, nine different cities served as the U.S. capital.

The original capital city was Philadelphia.

Then Baltimore took over in 1777—but shortly after, the capital was continually moved because of fighting in the Revolutionary War.

The capital was located in Lancaster and York, Pennsylvania, Trenton and Princeton, New Jersey, and Annapolis, Maryland

After the war, New York City became the capital, and then it was moved back to Philadelphia.

Finally, in 1790, a Congressional committee was appointed to select a permanent capital city—and the early favorite was Trenton.

But Southerners lobbied to place the capital in the South. Northerners argued for the North.

Alexander Hamilton and George Washington worked out a compromise, proposing that the capital be located in what was then about

177

The States

halfway between the North and South.

Maryland and Virginia agreed to give up part of their land to create a federal city—and in 1800, the U.S. government moved to its new home in Washington, D.C.

Congress was virtually unanimous in feeling the city should be named after George Washington.

The District, to differentiate it from a state, was named after Columbus, and called the District of Columbia.

SEVEN

Quotes on America

Seven

QUOTES ON AMERICA

I believe in America because in it we are free—free to choose our government, to speak our minds, to observe our different religions. Because we are generous with our freedom. Because we are blessed with natural and varied abundance. Because we have great dreams and because we have the opportunity to make those dreams come true.

Wendell Wilkie

America has never forgotten—and will never forget—the nobler things that brought her into being and that light her path.

Bernard Baruch

America, the land of unlimited possibilities.

Ludwig Goldberger

The Quotes

I always consider America with reverence and wonder, as the opening of a grand scene and design for mankind all over the earth.

John Adams

You cannot conquer America.

William Pitt

America is God's crucible, the great melting pot.

Israel Zangwill

Americans are the hope of this world.

Baron de l'Aulne

God bless America, land that I love.

Irving Berlin

The Quotes

America, God shed his grace on thee.
Katharine Lee Bates

Give me your tired, your poor...yearning to breathe free.
Emma Lazarus

We must preserve the sacred fire of liberty.
George Washington

I am a free man—an American.
Lyndon Johnson

The Quotes

If the American Revolution had produced nothing but the Declaration of Independence, it would have been worthwhile...The beauty and cogency of the preamble, reaching back to remotest antiquity and forward to an indefinite future, have lifted the hearts of millions of men and will continue to do...These words are more revolutionary than anything written by Robespierre, Marx, or Lenin, more explosive than the atom, a continual challenge to ourselves as well as an inspiration to the oppressed of all the world.

Samuel Eliot Morison

Join in hands, brave Americans all! By uniting we stand, by dividing we fall.

John Dickinson

I love Americans because they love liberty.

William Pitt

There is in most Americans some spark of idealism, which can be fanned into a flame. It takes sometimes a divining rod to find what it is; but when found, and that means often, when disclosed to the owners, the results are often extraordinary.

Justice Louis Brandeis

The American, by nature, is optimistic. He is experimental, an inventor and a builder who builds best when called upon to build greatly.

John F. Kennedy

The patriots are those who love America enough to see her as a model to mankind.

Adlai Stevenson

The Quotes

America is another name for opportunity. Our whole history appears like a last effort of divine Providence in behalf of the human race.

Ralph Waldo Emerson

To us Americans much as been given; of us much is required. With all our faults and mistakes, it is our strength in support of the freedom our forefathers loved which has saved mankind from subjection to totalitarian power.

Walter Lippman

Many reasons may be assigned for the amazing economic development of the United States...In my judgement the greatest factor has been...that there was created here in America the largest area in the world in which there were no barriers to the exchange of goods and ideas.

Wendell Wilkie

The genius of America is that it makes little difference where or when a man was born if he had this vivid sense of American history, if he has learned to put Country above Party...if freedom means more than personal security and if he refuses to tolerate appeasement of tyranny as the price of peace.

McIlyar H. Lichliter

The American's Creed

There was a contest in 1917 for the writing of an American Creed to exemplify "the best summary of the political faith in America."

Oddly enough, the winner of the nationwide contest was a man named Page—who had actually been a page in the U.S. House of Representatives. He was William Page.

Here's what Page wrote, which was adopted by Congress as the official American's Creed:

"I believe in the United States of America as a government of the people, by the people, for the people; whose just powers are derived from the consent of the governed; a democracy in a Republic; a sovereign Nation of many sovereign States; a perfect Union, one and inseparable; established upon those principles of freedom, equality, justice, and humanity for which American patriots sacrificed their lives and fortunes.

"I therefore believe it is my duty to my country to love it; to support its Constitution; to obey its laws; to respect its flag; and to defend it against all enemies."

Other books in the
Knowledge in a Nutshell®
series:

Knowledge in a Nutshell…astound your family and stump your friends with…the man who was present when THREE U.S. Presidents were assassinated…how the Oscars got their name …what were the biggest animals that ever lived (it wasn't the dinosaurs)…

Knowledge in a Nutshell on Sports…over 500 amazing fun facts…a treasure chest for sports trivia buffs…the great team that never existed…why golf courses have 18 holes…the six-inch home run.

Knowledge in a Nutshell on Popular Products Heinz Edition, things you never knew about …why ketchup is called "ketchup"…what popular food was first used as a medicine in 400 B.C.… plus international recipes and fun food facts.

Knowledge in a Nutshell® **food products:**
Knowledge in a Nutshell - The Edible Game-
The Smart Cookie
Knowledge in a Nutshell - Sweet Smarts—
The Candy with a Brain

Call 1-800-NUTSHELL (U.S./Canada only)
All others call 1-412-765-2020 or visit our Web site
www.knowledgeinanutshell.com

If you have an interesting fact, and the story behind it, for future *Knowledge in a Nutshell®* books, send it along. We pay $10 for every fact and its story that we use in the book – and we'll acknowledge you as the contributor. Please write us at:

Knowledge in a Nutshell, Inc.
1420 Centre Ave. Suite 2216
Pittsburgh, PA 15219 USA.

For bulk sales or other questions

Call 1-800-NUTSHELL (U.S./Canada only)
All others call 1-412-765-2020 or visit our
Web site
www.knowledgeinanutshell.com

NOTE:. Quantity discounts are available.

Printed in the United States
34846LVS00001B/20